The
CHOSEN

SEASON ONE

KIDS ACTIVITY BOOK

```
E F
H E
D U V W
G I N T X K
N C M A A S S
T O N G A L U V
Q K Z N P K X A N C
A I L A R T S U A E A H
B I E U V V C Q K F M Z V G
O V R A I N O D E L A C W E N
C G U S D N A L S I K O O C E E H
A A E N I U G W E N U A P A P B N K
S O L O M O N I S L A N D S H N F I J I
              H N
D N A L S I S A M T S I R H C C C P D D
N E F R E N C H P O L Y N E S I A I A I
L P A O M A S N R E T S E W Q X
A I T A B I R I K A W A J F
```

BroadStreet
KIDS

D1455825

BroadStreet Kids
Savage, Minnesota, USA

BroadStreet Kids is an imprint of BroadStreet Publishing®
Broadstreetpublishing.com

The
CHOSEN

Kids Activity Book: Season 1

© 2021 by The Chosen LLC

978-1-4245-6287-9

Design by Chris Garborg | garborgdesign.com
Created, edited, and compiled by Michelle Winger | literallyprecise.com
Mazes licensed from mazegenerator.net.

Printed in China.

21 22 23 24 25 26 27   7 6 5 4 3 2 1

Practice the first three letters of the Hebrew alphabet!

ALEF

This Hebrew letter is silent.

א

BET

This letter sounds like the **b** in boat.

ב

GIMEL

This letter sounds like the **g** in goat.

ג

RAISINS AND SPICE

USE THE LETTERS AND NUMBERS
TO SHOW WHERE EACH OF THESE
PIECES BELONG IN THE PUZZLE.
WE GOT YOU STARTED! ⟶ C6

_____ | _____ | _____

_____ | _____ | _____

_____ | _____ | _____

SECRET DECODER

Use the code below
to unscramble the
hidden message.

✦	☸	❖	🕊	●	⚑	🐕	□	✡	✝	⚷	✾	☾
A	B	C	D	E	F	G	H	I	J	K	L	M

◆	★	💰	▲	♫	☼	◗	✳	🗡	≋	✖	◎	※
N	O	P	Q	R	S	T	U	V	W	X	Y	Z

Answer on page 149

CROSSWORD FUN

Use the clues below to solve the crossword. Answers with multiple words are shown with brackets revealing how many letters are in each word.

ACROSS

3. What Lilith gave to Sol at The Hammer
6. Used for sleeping outside
8. The rabbi
9. What drew Lilith away from the cliff
10. What Matthew needed to get into the tax booth
11. Sea vessel used by fishermen (7, 4)
15. A group of people traveling across the desert together
16. The rabbi's wife
17. The prophet that Mary and her father quote
18. The praetor of Capernaum

DOWN

1. Mary's other name
2. Simon's wife
4. Simon's brother
5. Who Simon was fighting to earn money
7. The secret tavern (3, 6)
12. Mary's father
13. Ancient material used for writing on
14. The first five books of the Bible

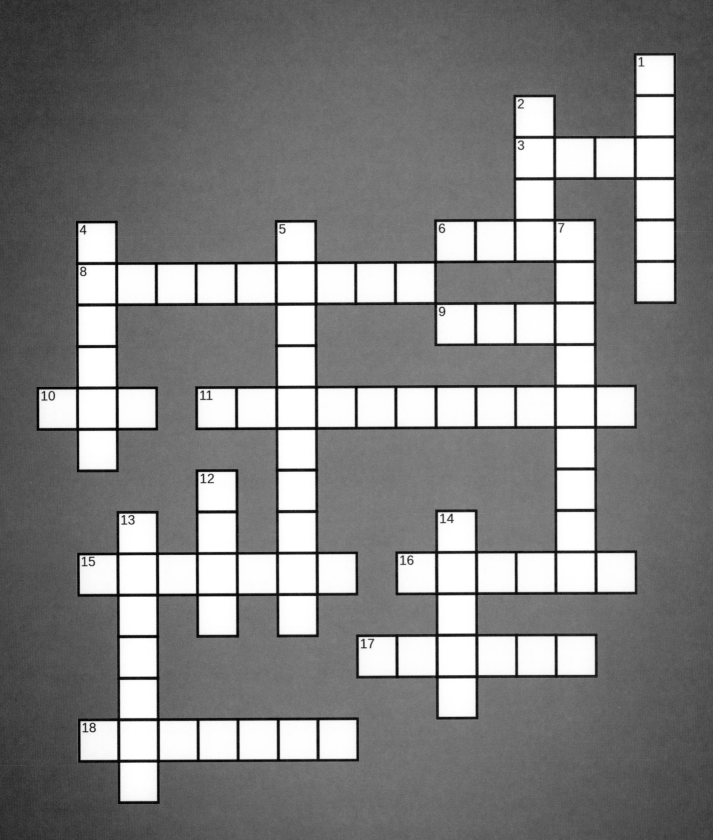

Answer on page 149

Find the following characters hidden in the word search puzzle.

Abrahim
Adonai
Andrew
Anna
Eden
Eema
Gaius
Isaiah
Jehosaphat
Jesus
Lilith
Marcus
Mary
Matthew
Nicodemus
Omar
Quintus
Rivka
Shmuel
Simon
Sol
Yussif
Zohara

```
                    D
                F   L   Q
                I   F   I   L
            A   I   H   A   L   M
            N   T   X   G   U   I   Y
        N   D   P   X   Z   Q   S   T   E
        Z   R   G   P   C   L   Q   T   H   M
        S   L   E   Q   P   S   M   D   W   V   V   U
        U   Y   W   S   U   N   W   H   Y   R   A   M   J
    T   I   P   Q   J   X   I   B   X   E   S   R   S   J   E
    I   A   V   C   S   C   J   N   E   G   Q   X   U   K   U   E
    I   L   G   H   G   T   F   B   M   T   Z   P   O   M   H   K   M   F
    M   Z   O   A   P   I   A   A   Y   T   U   H   G   E   V   H   K   J   U
    S   V   C   E   Y   B   A   J   V   D   U   U   S   E   D   L   B   W   F   L   A
    W   V   U   H   S   I   G   S   Z   M   E   U   E   A   O   C   C   E   I   F   N   N
X   O   C   Q   N   P   J   A   D   O   N   A   I   D   R   C   M   C   C   D   L   I   W   S
E   S   U   H   Z   O   H   A   R   A   H   C   D   P   O   I   T   M   A   R   C   U   S   O   L
N   O   G   E   Q   B   H   H   B   A   B   K   E   J   K   S   N   O   W   Y   G   B   U   A   S   Y   I
L   E   W   W   M   K   U   F   T   N   V   L   F   J   N   Z   C   M   I   H   A   R   B   A   I   U   N   C
C   A   B   E   Z   G   O   M   A   R   W   S   J   V   Y   X   S   J   J   W   O   P   V   F   D   U   A   Y   L   B
                    H
                    M
                    U
S   E   S   G   Q   N   D   U   H   S   D   E   M   G   Z   N   V   I   D   E   J   I   Y   A   N   Z   J   Z   P   E
Q   U   O   E   W   Y   J   E   A   A   L   S   I   M   O   N   V   N   E   A   B   S   D   E   A   Y   X   K
T   S   D   D   S   Q   U   M   E   S   K   K   G   K   I   U   I   D   V   R   Q   A   A   N   U   B   D   Q
    E   D   K   L   P   C   O   Q   S   I   V   R   L   U   K   X   Y   X   Z   N   X   J   I   X   T   S
    J   T   K   H   H   Z   U   I   M   I   M   I   I   M   M   C   U   V   N   O   Q   Z   Z   A   F   D
    M   A   T   T   H   E   W   M   H   L   Z   R   A   U   W   H   A   A   Z   W   Y   U   Q   H
```

AT THE MARKET

Match the definitions on the left with the words on the right.

Booths in the market	Scarves
Wholesale traders	Grapes
Goods sold at the market	Clay pots
A round red fruit with edible seeds	Rugs
People buying goods at the market	Stalls
Used to move and store market goods	Fish
They sit on the street asking for money	Wares
Popular fruit smashed to make wine	Sandals
Another name for a market	Jewelry
Decorative floor coverings	Shopkeeper
What Simon was trying to catch	Merchants
Weaved containers	Carts
Pear-shaped fruit often eaten dried	Pomegranates
Typical warm climate footwear	Baskets
A woman's head covering	Olives
A decorative accessory	Tote
Where liquids may be stored	Figs
A bag used to carry goods	Shoppers
Fruit used as a source of oil	Bazaar
Stall owner and seller of goods	Beggars

Answer on page 149

WORD FIT

The types of people listed below fit in the puzzle only one way. Use the number of letters in each word as a clue to where it could be placed. We have given you one to help you begin.

3 LETTERS
JEW

5 LETTERS
GUARD
ROMAN

6 LETTERS
ESSENE
PILATE
SAILOR
ZEALOT

7 LETTERS
PRAETOR
SERVANT
SOLDIER
STUDENT
TEACHER

8 LETTERS
MERCHANT
PHARISEE
SADDUCEE

9 LETTERS
CENTURION
FISHERMAN

10 LETTERS
FISHMONGER
MAGISTRATE
SHOPKEEPER

11 LETTERS
LEGIONNAIRE

14 LETTERS
GREAT SANHEDRIN

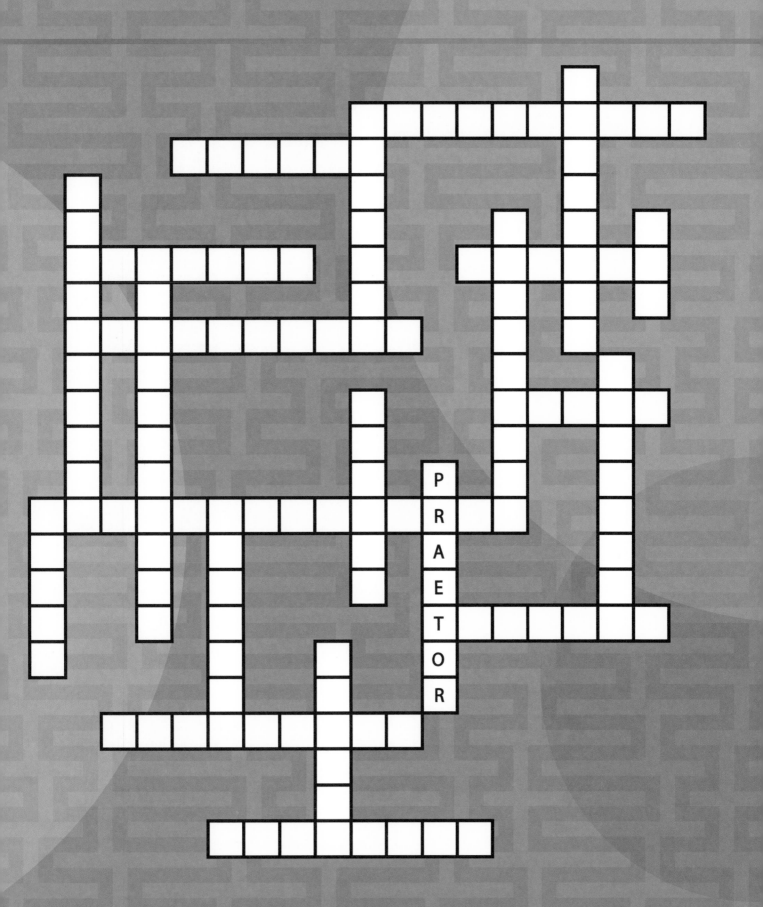

Answer on page 150

WORD (IN) WORD

The missing letters in each answer spell smaller words listed below. Use the clues to figure out the original word, putting the smaller words back in place. Use each word only once.

INN	ELM	CAGE
FILL	RINSE	SAND
TEN	WAS	GAME
BET	TALL	BARE
ROLL	WON	TIC
ACHE	EDGE	

Piece of clothing	_ _ R _ _ N T
Where a teacher puts lesson notes	L E C _ _ R _
Paper made from animal skin	P _ R _ _ M _ N T
Paper wrapped around handles	S C _ _ _ _
Market booths	S _ _ _ _ S
Goods sold at the market	_ _ R E _
Loose garment	_ U N _ _
Large container for liquids	_ _ R _ _ L S
Protective head covering	H _ _ _ E T
Fragrant perfume	F _ A N K _ _ C E N _ _
Typical hot climate shoes	_ _ _ _ A L S
Wheeled trailer for carrying goods	_ A G _ _
Boxed Jewish prayers	T E _ _ _ _ I N
Book of accounts	L _ _ _ _ R
Type of fabric	L _ _ E _
Carrying container	_ U C K _ _
Passenger vehicle pulled by horses	_ _ R R I A _ _

Answer on page 150

WORD SCRAMBLE

Unscramble the words to discover the animals seen or mentioned in Episode 1.

VODE _ _ _ _

ALMEC _ _ _ _ _

SOREH _ _ _ _ _

HIFS _ _ _ _

TARS _ _ _ _

SDRAENIS _ _ _ _ _ _ _ _

SIPG _ _ _ _ _

ODG _ _ _

Answer on page 150

Help Matthew get
to his tax booth!

How many bags of
coins does he collect
along the way?

_____

Answer on page 150

Start
here

Alphabet practice!

Practice the next three letters of the Hebrew alphabet!

DALET

ד

This letter sounds like the **d** in doll.

HE

ה

This letter sounds like the **h** in horse.

WAW

ו

This letter sounds like the **w** in well.

WHO AM I?

Match the definitions on the left with the people on the right.

the chief justice	saba
commander of a Roman army	dominus
rules over a court	rabbanit
grandmother	savta
Roman master	judge
entertainer who keeps objects in the air	abba
grandfather	juggler
contracted tax collector	eema
a person who arranges or cuts hair	publicanus
father	Av Beit Din
a rabbi's wife	blind person
someone who can't see	Sanhedrin
like the Supreme Court of Jewish history	hairdresser
mother	centurion

Answer on page 150

SCROLLS

USE THE LETTERS AND NUMBERS
TO SHOW WHERE EACH OF THESE
PIECES BELONG IN THE PUZZLE.
WE GOT YOU STARTED! ———————⟶

F5

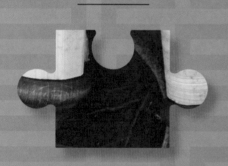

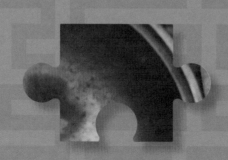

WORD FIT

The places listed below fit in the puzzle only one way. Use the number of letters in each word as a clue to where it could be put. We have given you one to help you begin.

3 LETTERS
ROME

5 LETTERS
ALLEY
HOUSE
JUDEA
SHORE

6 LETTERS
BAZAAR
DESERT
HOSTEL
MARKET
RAVINE
STREET

7 LETTERS
CYPRESS
MAGDALA

8 LETTERS
TAX BOOTH

9 LETTERS
CAPERNAUM
JERUSALEM
SYNAGOGUE
THE HAMMER
TORAH ROOM

10 LETTERS
RED QUARTER
WILDERNESS

11 LETTERS
BEDOUIN CAMP

12 LETTERS
AMPHITHEATER

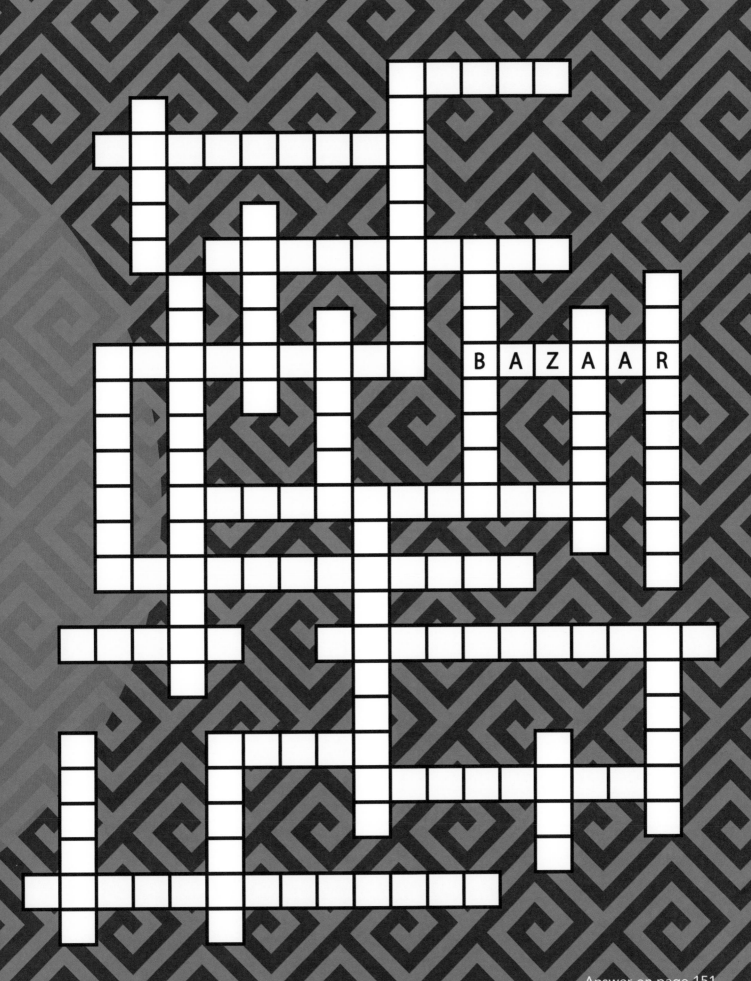

Answer on page 151

SECRET DECODER

Use the code below to unscramble a special Shabbat message.

✦	☸	❖	🕊	●	🚩	🐈	□	✡	✝	⚷	✾	☾
A	B	C	D	E	F	G	H	I	J	K	L	M

◆	★	💰	▲	♫	☼	◗	✳	🗡	〰	✖	◎	✻
N	O	P	Q	R	S	T	U	V	W	X	Y	Z

Answer on page 151

WORD PIECES

SHABBAT

Some words describing things about
Shabbat have fallen apart. Use the clues below
to piece them back together.
Each group of letters can only be used once.

PASS	STAR	DLES	LY	CAN
IR	ER	OVER	KID	IS
DUSH	RF	JAS	FRU	LOM
IT	SHA	SED	DENTS	DOG
MINE	STU	WEEK	SCA	FIRST

1. The ceremony of prayer and blessing. (7 letters)

   _____

2. What Mary goes in search of to finish the patron's hair. (7 letters)

   _____

3. The flower Mary puts on the table for Shabbat. (4 letters)

   _____

4. Type of food Gaius takes from the vendor without paying. (5 letters)

   _____

5. What Mary has in the box when she returns to the salon. (7 letters)

   _____

6. A customary Jewish greeting. (6 letters)

   _____

7. What Mary puts on when she runs into Nicodemus. (5 letters)

   _____

8. Who befriends Matthew on his way to Shabbat? (3 letters)

   _____

9. What were Little James and Thaddeus to Jesus? (8 letters)

   _____

10. When do you set an extra place for Elijah? (8 letters)

    _____

11. When is Passover held? (5 letters)

    _____

12. When do you begin the Shabbat meal? (2 words; 5 letters, 4 letters)

    _____

13. How often is Shabbat? (6 letters)

    _____

Answer on page 151

Find the following characters hidden in the word search puzzle.

Amos

Ananias

Barnaby

Baruch

Eli

Gideon

Haim

James

Jason

John

Jori

Lia

Little James

Mary Magdalene

Shula

Thaddeus

Tobiah

```
                              A D
                              I C
    A O                       L S                          I X
    Q B                       H P                          R D
    F G           Z M K C F A           O H
      T O B I A H R U N J K
      Q A X H E C F R O H
    C H Y Z C N L K L A E N
    S E M A J E I D T V B D
J T H A D D E U S L T U N N Z A I Y Q W
N G H X P E Q Q U A T N T H V D B G Y C
    C T L G D D L O S P O A
    S X R I E G E K X A N J
      O A W A A J G B R I
      L M H H M A J A S O N
    U V       A L Y M B L           O A
  H C               R E               Z N
S V                 A S               O A
                    M Z
                    K J
```

33

CROSSWORD FUN

Use the clues below to solve the crossword. Answers with more than one word are shown with brackets telling how many letters are in each word.

ACROSS

2. The first friend the little girl brought to the campsite
6. What Jesus was making with wood (4, 3)
7. Two things Jesus said wealthy people love (and 14 Down)
11. The name of the little girl's doll
12. What the little girl had to do before going out to play
15. The rabbi who said Jesus would be a great military leader

DOWN

1. Jesus said he especially loved this food
3. What Jesus was doing when all the children visited in the morning
4. What gift Jesus left for the little girl
5. Who Messiah would be most pleased with
8. The first child to visit the campsite
9. Jesus said this person provided everything he needed
10. The last thing Jesus did before going to sleep
13. What the little girl's mother wanted her to stay away from
14. See 7 Across

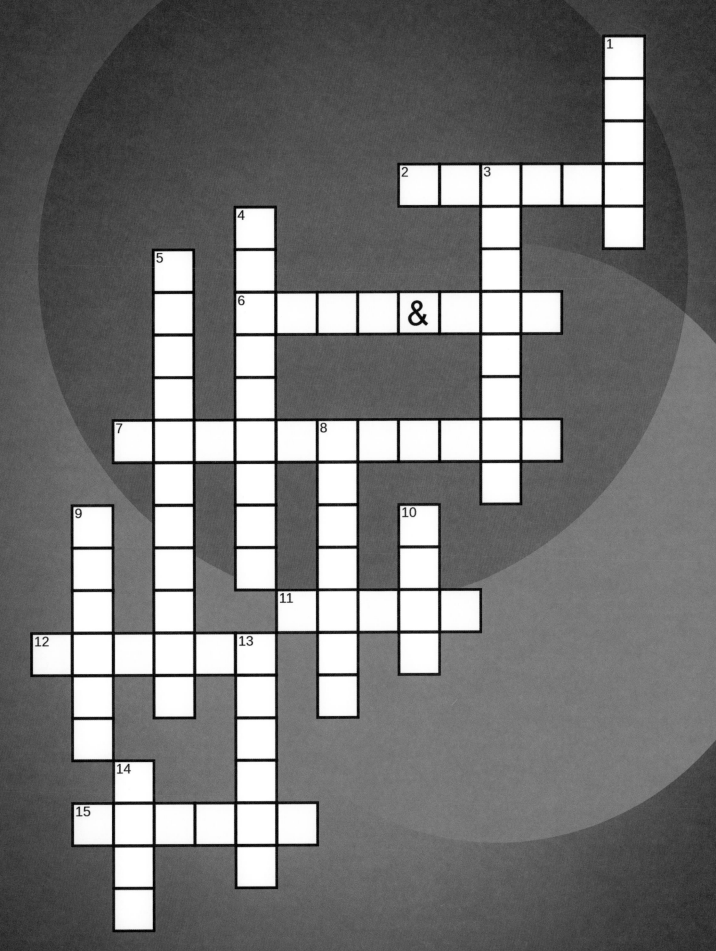

Answer on page 151

Scrambled Note

Jesus left a
note with his gift for Abigail,
but the letters got mixed up!
Unscramble each word so Abigail can read her card.

L I B A A I G ' I   W K O N

O Y U   A N C   D R A E .

U O Y   R A E   E V Y R

A C E P I S L '   H T I S

S T   O F R   Y U O .

I   I D D   T O N   M O E C

N L Y O   R O F   H E T

T A H E W L Y .

Alphabet practice!

ZAYIN

ז

This letter sounds like the **z** in Zebedee.

HET

ח

This letter sounds like the **ch** in Bach.

TET

ט

This letter sounds like the **t** in tax.

OLIVE IT

USE THE LETTERS AND NUMBERS
TO SHOW WHERE EACH OF THESE
PIECES BELONG IN THE PUZZLE.
WE GOT YOU STARTED! ⟶

C8

_____   _____   _____

_____   _____   _____

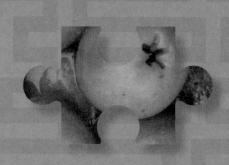

Use the code to unscramble the Shema.

✦	⚙	❖	🕊	●	⚑	🐏	□	✡	✝	🗝	❀	☾
A	B	C	D	E	F	G	H	I	J	K	L	M

◆	★	💰	➤	♫	✿	💧	❇	🗡	〜	✖	◎	※
N	O	P	Q	R	S	T	U	V	W	X	Y	Z

HEAR, ISRAEL,

THE LORD IS

OUR GOD, THE

LORD IS ONE.

YOU SHALL LOVE THE LORD YOUR

THE LORD YOUR GOD YOUR

GOD WITH ALL YOUR

YOUR HEART,

ALL YOUR SOUL,

AND ALL YOUR

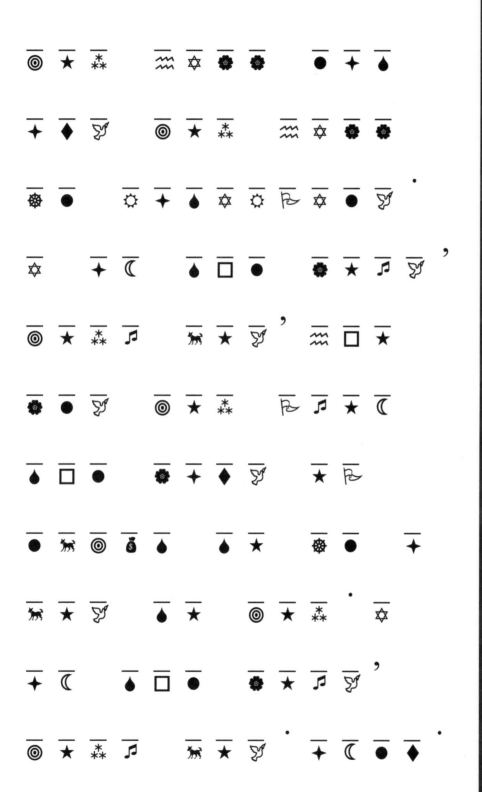

WORD CHANGE

Change the word CLAY into BOWL one letter at a time. Use the clues to help you figure out each word.

C L A Y

_ _ _ _   smack hands together

_ _ _ _   trim with scissors

_ _ _ _   potato slice

_ _ _ _   cut wood

_ _ _ _   chicken cage

_ _ _ _   cold

_ _ _ _   lacks common sense

_ _ _ _   bird

B O W L

Answer on page 152

MAZE

Help each person find their way to the Shabbat meal at Mary's house without crossing each other's paths.

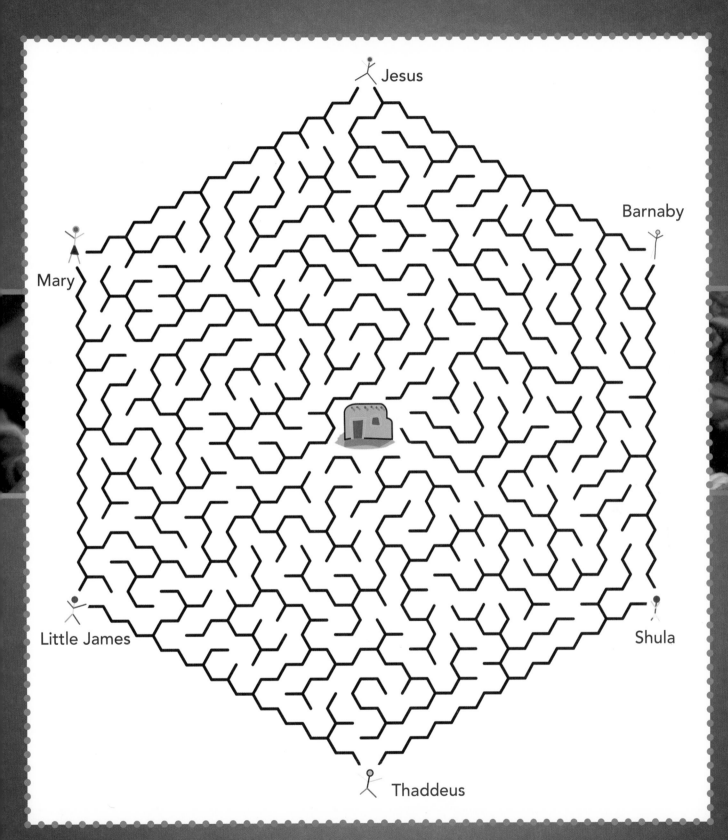

MIXED LETTERS

Use the code below to unscramble a special Scripture recited during Shabbat.

A	B	C	D	E	F	G	H	I	J	K	L	M
S	G	W	O	B	K	X	T	C	P	I	V	F

N	O	P	Q	R	S	T	U	V	W	X	Y	Z
A	R	Z	M	Q	D	N	J	E	Y	H	L	U

B̄ D̄ S̄   Ē Ȳ V̄ Ā Ā V̄ S̄

H̄ X̄ V̄   Ā V̄ L̄ V̄ T̄ H̄ X̄

S̄ N̄ W̄   N̄ T̄ S̄   Q̄ N̄ S̄ V̄

K̄ H̄   X̄ D̄ Ȳ W̄ ’   M̄ D̄ Ō

D̄ T̄   K̄ H̄   X̄ V̄

Ō V̄ Ā H̄ V̄ S̄   M̄ Ō D̄ Q̄

N̄ Ȳ Ȳ   X̄ K̄ Ā   C̄ D̄ Ō F̄ .

Answer on page 152

WORD (IN) WORD

Who Is this Man?

The children talked about who Jesus was. Put the small words back in place using the clues and discover some of the things the children thought Jesus might be. Use each small word only once. Then, put the letters in the blue circles in order below to find out who Abigail said Jesus was.

FAN   TEAR   CAPE   RIM   TOGA   POET   BIDE   MUD

A person who builds with wood

_ ○R _ E N T _ R
  7

A person skilled in a craft

C R A _ T S M _ ○
                8

A person with a lot of strength

S _ R ○N ○M _ N
     4   2

A person who passes on knowledge

_ _ ○C H E _
    1

A person who speaks for God

_ R ○P H _ _
     3

A person who creates by joining items

_ U _ L ○_ R
        5

A person who kills someone

○_ R _ E R E R
 6

A person who breaks the law

C _ _ _ I N A L

Who Abigail said Jesus was:

   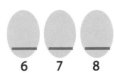

1   2   3   4   5   6   7   8

Answer on page 152

At the Campsite

Find the following campsite items hidden in the word search puzzle.

Animal skins
Blanket
Branches
Bread
Canopy
Cloak
Fire pit
Fish
Food
Fruit
Grapes
Knapsack
Knife

Legumes
Pots
Rocks
Stew
Tables
Tent
Tools
Torches
Tree stumps
Utensils
Vegetables
Wood

X S D K T G L   P E R V A Z R
N M W E H T N T   L H W O O D R X
G H S N B T O F B   C X N Q X W Z   U B
Z T Q T P N O O L R M S Y R H G L D S X
T E A F B O I L K E S T I P E R I F E L
B K A O L C N S T A U Q V I O U B K H G
Z N Q X V T I N D D Y A C R D N V S C X
Q A W N B H E I R C S O X U E Y R A F R K
A L R K V N P K X J U T E N S I L S C O C
B T J T N A S S P M U T S E E R T X T
D L P B S H K E I   H K E I
S D U L S R A V P U T F I E C E Y E F
L E G U M E S M E Z P I O K N A P S A C K
C P J F K P R I G S N N S P G O G A R F A
D A Y L I F L N E K E R D Y O N A O Z N J
L R Z R R S Q A T U   L S S E H C N A R B
P G F U X V H J A N   M B Z W J P S M R I
U D I D A U Z H B C   V A A T E H J O I Z
H T X P K A I L D   S R N T M T C   Q Y
J U Q B W Y E Z   D S Q Q L K S B
F O O D J P S   B S N S S J Y

The Larger Job

Jesus told the children they had a larger job to do. What four jobs did he say they needed to take care of?

Use the grid below to figure out which letters go where, so you can read the job list too! We have given you some letters to start.

			Q	C			L				X	
1	2	3	4	5	6	7	8	9	10	11	12	13

J	E					B			Z	P		H
14	15	16	17	18	19	20	21	22	23	24	25	26

CODE

Answer on page 152

1

___ ___ ___ ___   ___ ___ ___ ___   ___ ___
6   26   13   3   8   13   18   15   21   13

___ ___ ___ ___ ___ ___ .
13   21   26   15   9   6

2

___ ___ ___ ___   ___ ___ ___   ___   ___ ___ ___ ___ ,
21   11   19   15   22   13   17   6   3   13   9   17

___ ___ ___   ___ ___ ___ ___ ___   ___ ___ .
11   1   17   6   26   11   9   15   2   21

3

___ ___ ___ ___ ___   ___ ___ ___ ___
26   13   1   13   9   10   13   16   9

___ ___ ___ ___ ___ ___   ___ ___ ___
7   11   21   26   15   9   11   1   17

___ ___ ___ ___ ___ ___ .
25   13   21   26   15   9

4

___ ___ ___ ___   ___ ___ ___   ___ ___ ___ ___
8   13   18   15   21   26   15   8   13   9   17

___ ___ ___ ___   ___ ___ ___   ___ ___ ___ ___
10   13   16   9   22   13   17   3   2   21   26

___ ___ ___   ___ ___ ___ ___   ___ ___ ___ ___ ___ .
11   8   8   10   13   16   9   26   15   11   9   21

WORD CHANGE

Change the word CAMP into WOOD one letter at a time. Use the clues to help you figure out each word.

C A M P

_ _ _ _   type of fish

_ _ _ _   show concern

_ _ _ _   price of a travel ticket

_ _ _ _   burning material

_ _ _ _   at the front

_ _ _ _   shallow part of a river

_ _ _ _   something you eat

W O O D

Answer on page 152

WHOSE FISH?

Follow the line to find out who catches the fish.

SIMON   ANDREW   JAMES   JOHN

Answer on page

Why Are You Here?

Beginning with the first row, circle the words you find going across only (and not backwards). Then move down to the next row and continue finding words. When you have finished circling all the words in the puzzle, write them on the lines and you will discover what Jesus told the children his purpose on earth was.

_____

_____

_____

_____

_____

_____

_____

```
T H E F R T S P I R I T X M O Y O F R L T
L M P T H E B U X N L O R D N L R I S P F
U P O N H R M E C B E C A U S E G R H E Q
W I H A S N X A N O I N T E D P L M E Q A
S T O L P R O C L A I M N R D L G O O D I
F H M N E W S R I Q N T O C G T H E P N R
P O O R L G H E C T H A S M R L S E N T P
S N T M E G R M S T T O B P R O C L A I M
T X L I B E R T Y I R L F T O B N T H E T
I C A P T I V E S R Y T E P D A N D F R L
P H R M O L R E C O V E R I N G T X O F R
S I G H T E Q P R L T O L M T H E T C L P
R C H B L I N D N H T P T O Q R S S E T T
U A T V H L I B E R T Y W A B T H O S E B
W H O Q R T H S A R E L N P R N Q T H L S
C T X O P P R E S S E D T B L T O S F R Q
A B D M C P R T F A P R O C L A I M T P O
G T H E Q N G Y E A R L T F I O F H R L M
T H E B T L O R D S C H R F A V O R T X F
```

Answer on page 153

WORD FIND

HORSING AROUND

USE THE LETTERS AND NUMBERS
TO SHOW WHERE EACH OF THESE
PIECES BELONG IN THE PUZZLE.
WE GOT YOU STARTED! ——————→ C8

_____

_____

_____

_____

_____

_____

_____

_____

Answer on page 153

WORD FIT

The water words listed below fit in the puzzle only one way. Use the number of letters in each word as a clue to where it could be put. We have given you one to help you begin.

3 LETTERS
ROW
SEA
SKY
SUN

4 LETTERS
MOON
ROCK
SAIL
WAVE

5 LETTERS
BEACH
CHURN
FROTH
GLIDE
SHORE
STARS

TRAWL
WATER

6 LETTERS
GURGLE
PADDLE
SPLASH

7 LETTERS
GLISTEN
HORIZON
SPARKLE

Answer on page 153

Alphabet practice!

Practice the next three letters of the Hebrew alphabet!

YOD

This letter sounds like the **y** in you.

KAF

This letter sounds like the **k** in key.

LAMED

This letter sounds like the **l** in love.

WORD CHANGE

Change the word FISH into MEAL one letter at a time. Use the clues to help you figure out each word.

F I S H

_ _ _ _   hope for

_ _ _ _   clean

_ _ _ _   crush to eat

_ _ _ _   holds the sail

_ _ _ _   the largest amount

_ _ _ _   water around a castle

_ _ _ _   food from animals

M E A L

Answer on page 153

FOLLOW THE LINE

Gone Fishing

The letters in these fishing words have gone missing. Use the letters in the fish to solve the puzzle. Each letter can be used more than once, but if there is a line between empty boxes, the same letter must be in those boxes. We have placed some letters to help you begin.

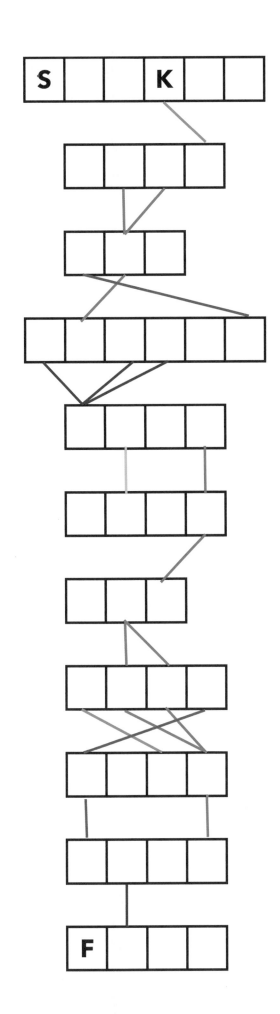

Answer on page 154

WORD (IN) WORD

All Aboard!

Use the definitions to figure out the words. The letters in the small words will help you figure out the big words. We've started the first one for you.

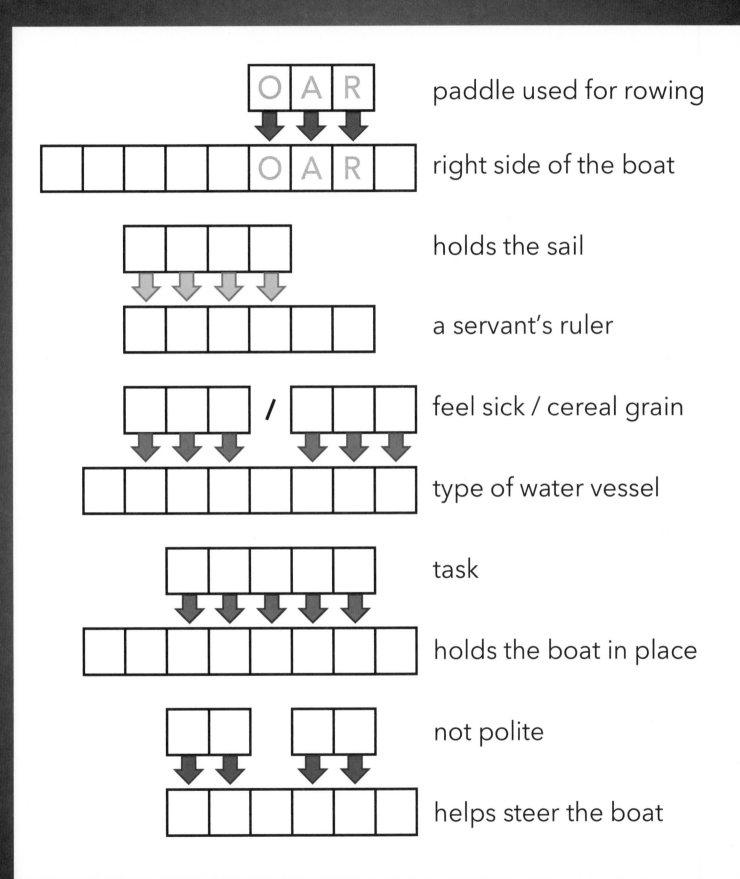

| O | A | R | | paddle used for rowing

right side of the boat

holds the sail

a servant's ruler

feel sick / cereal grain

type of water vessel

task

holds the boat in place

not polite

helps steer the boat

CROSSWORD FUN

Use the clues below to solve the crossword. Answers with more than one word are shown with brackets telling how many letters are in each word.

ACROSS

2. How many men were fishing in the fleet on Shabbat
3. What Simon said he lost at the docks
5. Who Andrew told Simon he had seen
8. What Jesus asked Simon to do (6, 2)
9. Part of Simon's body the soldier cut
12. The "crazy" man Nicodemus went to visit in prison (4, 3, 7)
13. The father Simon found fishing on Shabbat

DOWN

1. A "Z" was found on this piece of fishing equipment
3. What John called Jesus (4, 2, 3)
4. What the fisherman pulled from the water thinking it was a large catch
6. Roman leader trying to catch Simon
7. What the other fisherman called Simon
10. How many fish Simon caught before Jesus showed up
11. Man hired to report Simon's actions
14. Who guarded the tax booth when Matthew was away

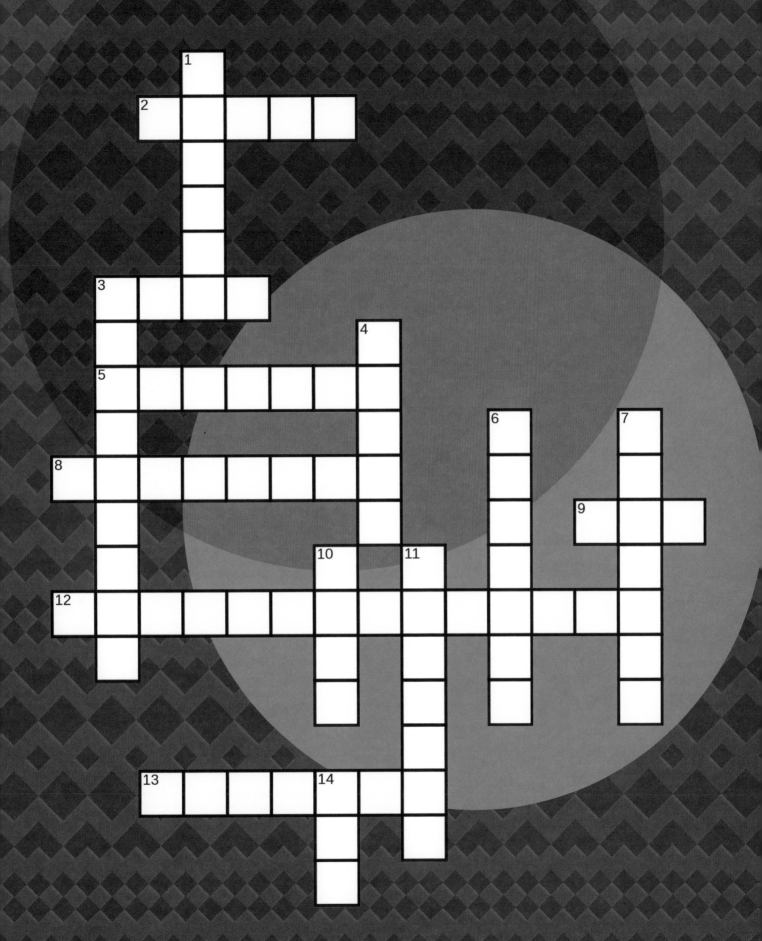

Answer on page 154

Alphabet practice!

Practice the next three letters of the Hebrew alphabet!

MEM

This letter sounds like the **m** in market.

NUN

This letter sounds like the **n** in net.

SAMEKH

This letter sounds like the **s** in sea.

WORD CHANGE

Change the word WATER into WINE one letter at a time. Use the clues to help you figure out each word.

W A T E R

_ _ _ _ _ a bet

Uh-oh! Lost a letter!

_ _ _ _ salary

_ _ _ _ walk in shallow water

_ _ _ _ large from side to side

W I N E

Answer on page 154

71

MAZE

John the Baptist

Find your way through the maze. As you pass through a letter, write it down and discover where John the Baptist spent a long time.

_ _ _ _ _ _ _ _ _ _ _

Answer on page 154

Start here

End here

WORD FIT

The words listed below fit in the puzzle only one way. Use the number of letters in each word as a clue to where it could be put. We have given you one word to help you begin.

4 LETTERS
CANA
CART
JUGS

5 LETTERS
CRATE
FLUTE
MYRRH
PLATE
TABLE

6 LETTERS
DONKEY
GOBLET
WATER

7 LETTERS
BANQUET
CHUPPAH

GALILEE
INCENSE
PLATTER
VINTAGE
WEDDING

8 LETTERS
CEREMONY
VINEYARD

9 LETTERS
COURTYARD
SYNAGOGUE

10 LETTERS
TAMBOURINE

11 LETTERS
COBBLESTONE
WILDFLOWERS

At a Wedding

M Y R R H

Answer on page

GOBS OF GOBLETS

USE THE LETTERS AND NUMBERS TO SHOW WHERE EACH OF THESE PIECES BELONG IN THE PUZZLE. WE GOT YOU STARTED! ⟶ C1

CROSSWORD FUN

Use the clues below to solve the crossword puzzle.

ACROSS

3. Who Jesus' mother said he was supposed to be with
6. A smart group of people who study
8. Jesus' earthly dad
9. What town Jesus' family was in when Jesus went missing
12. Chief synagogue official
13. Where Jesus was found
14. A large meal prepared for a celebration

DOWN

1. What a traveling group of people was called
2. Who Jesus said he was with
4. What Jesus was doing when his dad found him
5. What Jesus' family had come to town for
7. How many days it had been when Jesus' family finally found him
10. A person who made copies of written work
11. Jesus' mother
13. How old Jesus was when his parents lost him

Answer on page 155

At the Wedding

Find the people at the wedding in Cana hidden in the word search puzzle.

Abner

Andrew

Asher

Big James

Dinah

Helah

James

Jesus

John

Kafni

Mary

Mary Magdalene

Rafi

Ramah

Sarah

Simon

Thaddeus

Thomas

Tirza

```
        B F Z K T A T          C Q A J N G H
        K W C F L H W R        P W M X A Q N X
    U B   D H R A C P P        D I N A H N B     F U
    N J M G I D J V T B        S J O Z S V D Z G G
    H A T K D P E M S X        I H F X G E R R T K
    H A L E H G P N M U        M B C F T A M Q E S
    D R U F T C S F E Y        O R W S F F H A M W
    B S P F J H K T T L        K N W O I I R A O J M
    F T F Z P Z O Q S U        A R P B G J G O G G T
    V U J E S E M Y S R        D F X J P Z K T Y
          D G A Q E I G E D
        P X J A O E K X S L M S A Q N H B U O
    P U R S R G D Y R A M U A M M B E D W C W
    Z K H A F Y T B I G S O V J M Y F D J I L
    M E C P J R J H C V U X B U G J R O S W W
    R D Z W E W L A X R      N D N Q I H A G F J
    E A C N C I R R F O      I F E P N B Q M I M
    D R B V Q L F A P Q      U N T J J R A M A H
    A A   F U E W S I U      K K F W W U V     F B
        V C I T I R Z A      X E V A F K L E
        M D Q N T V W        V G F K P I P
```

Who Ate What?

Figure out who ate what meal at the wedding in Cana by following the lines.

Simon _____

Andrew _____

Thaddeus _____

Mary _____

James _____

John _____

Big James _____

Jesus _____

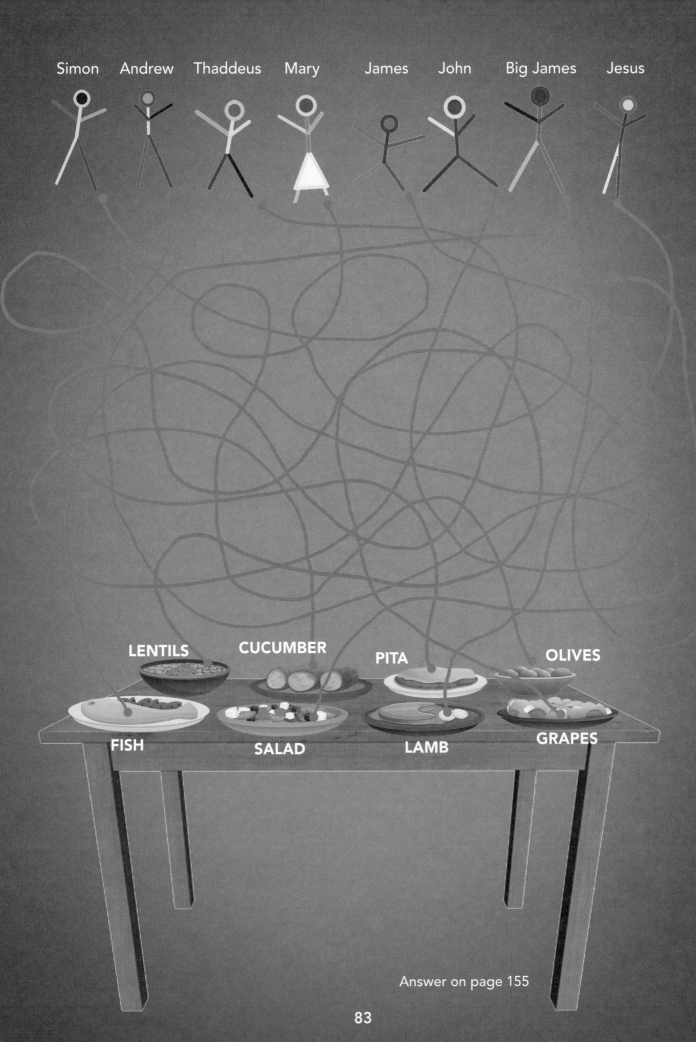

Answer on page 155

Time to Eat

The letters in some popular foods have gone missing. Use the letters in the olives to solve the puzzle. Each letter can be used more than once, but if there is a line between empty boxes, the same letter must be used in those boxes. We have placed some letters to help you begin.

Find the Hebrew letters hidden
in the marketplace pictures.

אבגדהוזחטיכלמנסעפצקרשת

Answer on page 156

MAZE

Lost in Jerusalem

Jesus stayed behind when the caravan with his family moved out. Mary and Joseph came back to Jerusalem searching frantically. Help Mary and Joseph find Jesus.

SECRET
DECODER

WHAT IS
HIS NAME?

Use the code below to
unscramble John the Baptist's
answer to Nicodemus.

✦	⛭	❖	🕊	●	⚑	🐏	□	✡	✝	⚷	✿	☾
A	B	C	D	E	F	G	H	I	J	K	L	M

◆	★	💰	▲	♫	☼	◉	❋	🗡	〰	✖	◎	※
N	O	P	Q	R	S	T	U	V	W	X	Y	Z

Answer on page 156

Alphabet practice!

Practice the next three letters of the Hebrew alphabet!

AYIN

This Hebrew letter is silent.

PE

This letter sounds like the **p** in pot.

TSADI

This letter sounds like the **ts** in eats.

WORD CHANGE

Change the word LAME into WALK one letter at a time.
Use the clues to help you figure out each word.

L A M E

_ _ _ _   body of water

_ _ _ _   create

_ _ _ _   boy

_ _ _ _   group of stores

_ _ _ _   barrier

W A L K

Answer on page 156

LOTS OF POTS

USE THE LETTERS AND NUMBERS
TO SHOW WHERE EACH OF THESE
PIECES BELONG IN THE PUZZLE.
WE GOT YOU STARTED! ⟶ A8

CROSSWORD FUN

Use the clues below to solve the crossword puzzle.

ACROSS

3. The teacher's pet
4. The boy on the roof
7. Eden's mother
9. He gave the leper his cloak
11. What Jesus' father was
14. The tax collector
15. Where the lame man entered the house

DOWN

1. What job the man with sores had
2. He had a great singing voice
5. The girl on the roof
6. Who the Egyptians brought to Jesus
8. He can't dance
10. Zebedee's wife
12. The Egyptian woman they met on the road
13. He was healed on the road

Answer on pa

At Zebedee's House

Many people watched the paralytic man get healed at Zebedee's house! Find some of the people who were there in the word search.

Abigail
Andrew
Barnaby
Big James
Deborah
Egyptians
Eliel
Gaius
James

Jesus
John
Joshua
Mara
Marcus
Mary
Nicodemus
Paralytic
Salome

Shmuel
Shula
Simon
Tamar
Thaddeus
Yussif
Zebedee

```
                        M
                      A V Z
                    R A Q B E
                  A K K I Q S B
                O Z V G V T X I E
              Q N O J S H R Y Q P D
            Y E T A Q D V G D Q H G E
          A I S M N I C O D E M U S K E
        L O Y E C P P T J O B W Z U I R T
      U B M S T S K R T U G O Q X F Y Z O Y
    H Q T G A I U S D A U Y R A B T E M R Y F
  S T L D L S T Z C P M X K A G R D V A E D B X
F C F X Y U S S I F I A I H H R F I M B W W C K B
Z L Z H P U V M X B B B R B U Q M W O A U H S O J G Z
L L H Y H N X J S S G K W E G Y P T I A N S S C P J B R G

    C H K E       D L U O R           W B Z M
    L D E J       J X G A D           I R V B
    M G L W       U Q G N F           U H K R
    F J I O       C U N L F           W G G B
    D M E T       L D Q R I           X A A T
    D A L N V Q Q E S E H B U A X U G X R K Q
    W J A O E X U U O Y S M A I G H N N J O P
    I Q R M O M G H U W U A I W I I A K E M K
    R T I I H U X K H Y S M W P E B B S K M N
    B I G S       T Z E X S S Y Q Y A E A L
    O F G F       Z M J X A G E U F T D R E
    B C V Q       G A D L N N         T C X
    D T I O       K Q O N I N         L U C
    E T V T       V M W Y Q W         M S A
    J W H Z Y I A M E I Z D O W       X I D
    A U P M C L Z R Q L F O E W   O   N J C
    M I W S E C A L K B K R W L       T N Z
    E A L V L R E R S H D C E V       X H E
    S T P X B W Y R A N G U S B       N O Q
    T H A D D E U S A P A X S N       N J P
```

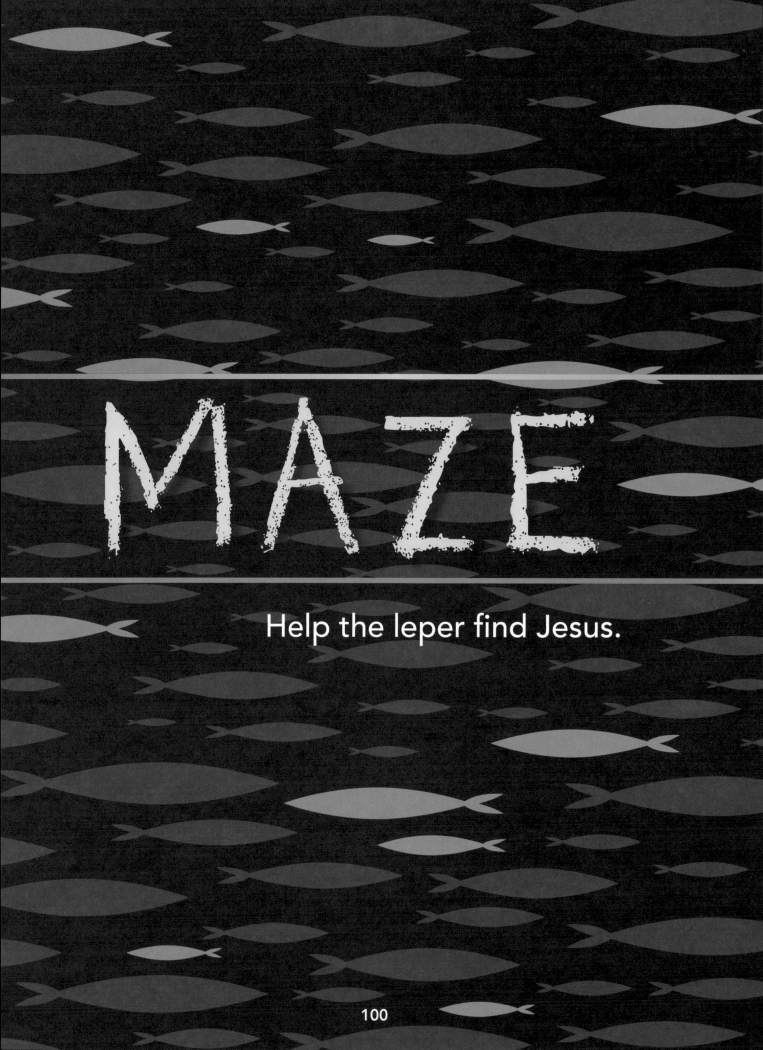

MAZE

Help the leper find Jesus.

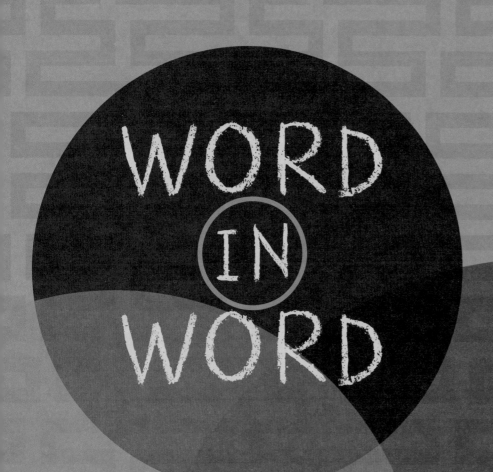

WORD (IN) WORD

In Salome's Kitchen

Use the definitions to figure out the words. The letters in the small words will help you figure out the big words. We've started the first one for you.

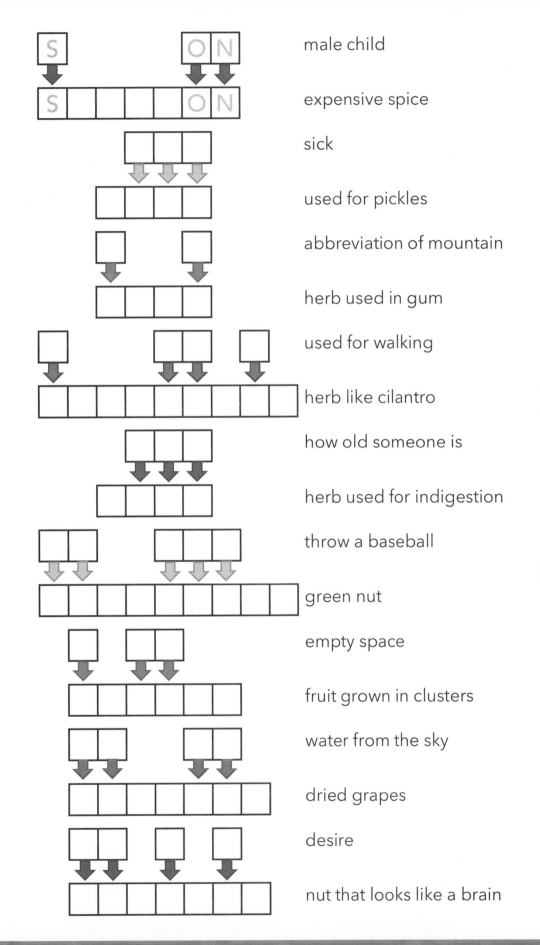

S			O	N	male child

S _ _ _ _ O N — expensive spice

_ _ _ — sick

_ _ _ _ — used for pickles

_ _ — abbreviation of mountain

_ _ _ _ — herb used in gum

_ _ _ — used for walking

_ _ _ _ _ _ _ _ — herb like cilantro

_ _ _ — how old someone is

_ _ _ _ — herb used for indigestion

_ _ _ _ — throw a baseball

_ _ _ _ _ _ _ _ _ — green nut

_ _ _ — empty space

_ _ _ _ _ _ _ — fruit grown in clusters

_ _ _ _ — water from the sky

_ _ _ _ _ _ _ — dried grapes

_ _ _ _ — desire

_ _ _ _ _ _ _ — nut that looks like a brain

Answer on page 157

NUMBER

Jesus told the crowd a story about servants needing to have their lamps ready for the master's return. Why was the story also important for us?

Use the grid below to figure out which letters go where so you can read the answer! We have given you some numbers to start.

Lamps Ready

A	B	C	D	E	F	G	H	I	J	K	L	M
		10							21			

N	O	P	Q	R	S	T	U	V	W	X	Y	Z
8		6	17	1					26			24

CODE

$\overline{8}\ \overline{2}\ \overline{3}\ \overline{7}\ \overline{11}\ \overline{2}\ \overline{1}\qquad\overline{7}\ \overline{11}\ \overline{2}\qquad\overline{5}\ \overline{8}\ \overline{19}\ \overline{2}\ \overline{23}\ \overline{12}$

$\overline{3}\ \overline{8}\qquad\overline{11}\ \overline{2}\ \overline{5}\ \overline{13}\ \overline{2}\ \overline{8}\qquad\overline{8}\ \overline{20}\ \overline{1}\qquad\overline{7}\ \overline{11}\ \overline{2}$

$\overline{12}\ \overline{20}\ \overline{8}\qquad\overline{20}\ \overline{25}\qquad\overline{4}\ \overline{5}\ \overline{8}\qquad\overline{16}\ \overline{8}\ \overline{20}\ \overline{9}$

$\overline{7}\ \overline{11}\ \overline{2}\qquad\overline{18}\ \overline{5}\ \overline{15}\qquad\overline{20}\ \overline{1}\qquad\overline{7}\ \overline{11}\ \overline{2}$

$\overline{11}\ \overline{20}\ \overline{22}\ \overline{1}\ ,\qquad\overline{14}\ \overline{22}\ \overline{7}\qquad\overline{20}\ \overline{8}\ \overline{23}\ \overline{15}\qquad\overline{7}\ \overline{11}\ \overline{2}$

$\overline{25}\ \overline{5}\ \overline{7}\ \overline{11}\ \overline{2}\ \overline{1}\ \cdot\qquad\overline{12}\ \overline{20}\qquad\overline{15}\ \overline{20}\ \overline{22}$

$\overline{4}\ \overline{22}\ \overline{12}\ \overline{7}\qquad\overline{5}\ \overline{23}\ \overline{9}\ \overline{5}\ \overline{15}\ \overline{12}\qquad\overline{14}\ \overline{2}$

$\overline{1}\ \overline{2}\ \overline{5}\ \overline{18}\ \overline{15}\ \cdot$

Answer on page 157

WORD FIT

The words listed below fit in the puzzle only one way. Use the number of letters in each word as a clue to where it could be put. We have given you one word to help you begin.

4 LETTERS
CANA
ROME
TYRE

5 LETTERS
EGYPT
JUDEA
SIDON
SINAI

6 LETTERS
CANAAN
JORDAN
SILOAM

7 LETTERS
CYPRESS
MAGDALA
SHECHEM

8 LETTERS
ETHIOPIA
NAZARETH

9 LETTERS
BETHLEHEM
CAPERNAUM
JERUSALEM
PHOENICIA

10 LETTERS
GENNESARET
HELIOPOLIS
THE DEAD SEA

12 LETTERS
SEA OF GALILEE

Places to Go

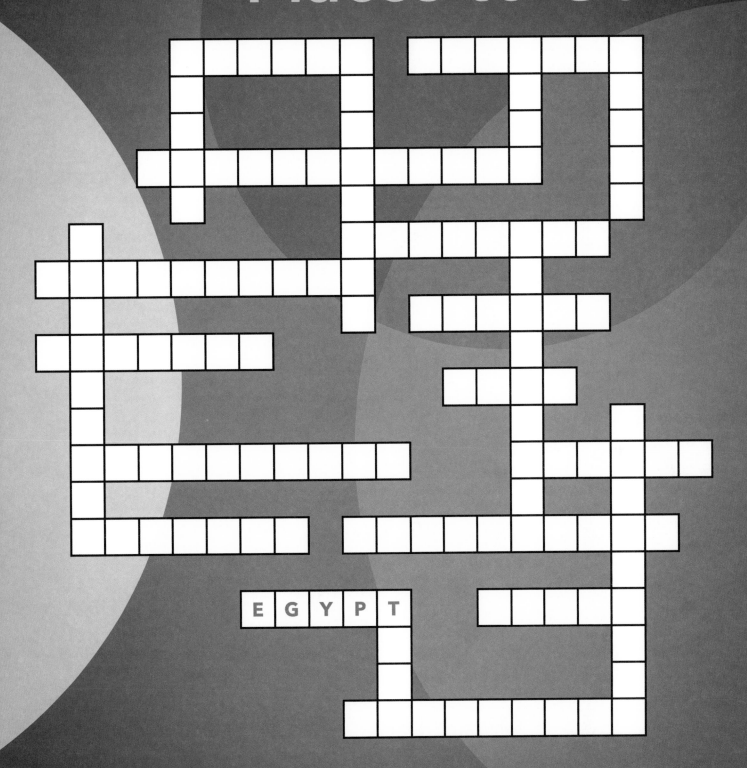

E G Y P T

Answer on page 157

SECRET DECODER

Use the code below to
unscramble what Jesus told
the crowd about praying.

✦	☸	❖	🕊	●	⚑	🐏	□	✡	✝	⚷	✿	☾
A	B	C	D	E	F	G	H	I	J	K	L	M

◆	★	💰	▲	♫	☼	◗	✳	🗡	〰	✖	◎	※
N	O	P	Q	R	S	T	U	V	W	X	Y	Z

Answer on page 158

HIDDEN MESSAGE

Beginning with the first row, circle the words you find going across only (and not backwards). When you have finished circling all the words, you will see what Jesus said. The leftover letters should be placed in the "Hidden Message" box for you to discover what Jesus was saying.

___ _____ ___ ____ ____ ___ ___ _____.

__ ____ ____ ____ ____ __ ___.

C O N S I D E R G H O W O T H E D L
W I L D O F L O W E R S V G R O W E
T H E Y S D O Y N O T O L A B O R U
O R M S P I N O Y E T R I E T E L L
T Y O U H N O T A E V E N N K I N G
Y S O L O M O N O U D R E S S E D C
A S A B E A U T I F U L L Y N I F I
T H A T M I S A H O W G G O D I N E
C L O T H E S H T H E E G R A S S W
O F I T H E L F I E L D L W H I C H
T I S A H E R E K T O D A Y E A N D
T O M O R R O W G I S O T H R O W N
O I N T O D T H E C F I R E A H O W
R M U C H E M O R E O W I L L F H E
Y C L O T H E O Y O U U ? ☺ ☺ ☺ ☺ ☺

Answer on page 158

WHICH FLAME

Fan into Flame

Jesus encouraged his disciples to show others his light. Put the words in the flames in the spaces below to complete the sentences Jesus spoke.

Our _____ isn't _____ we _____ and _____ to _____.

_____ are the _____ of the _____.

A _____ on a _____ _____ be _____.

Answer on page 158

cannot

You

some-thing

world

hidden

Faith

light

keep

hill

our-selves

hide

city

Alphabet practice!

Practice the next two letters of the Hebrew alphabet!

QOF

ק

This letter sounds like the **k** in kick.

RESH

ר

This letter sounds like the **r** in rabbi.

WORD CHANGE

DEAD

_ _ _ _   small round object

_ _ _ _   force into a curve

_ _ _ _   group of musicians

_ _ _ _   without hair

_ _ _ _   round sports object

_ _ _ _   border structure

_ _ _ _   a welt

_ _ _ _   trickery

_ _ _ _   spouse

LIFE

Answer on page 158

THE FRUIT MARKET

USE THE LETTERS AND NUMBERS
TO SHOW WHERE EACH OF THESE
PIECES BELONG IN THE PUZZLE.
WE GOT YOU STARTED! ———————→ F8

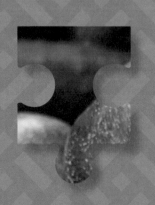

Answer on page 158

CROSSWORD FUN

Use the clues below to solve the crossword.

ACROSS

1. Who held up the bronze serpent
3. The disciple who was taking notes in the stairwell
5. Who Matthew gave the tax booth key to when he joined the disciples
8. Matthew's mother
9. Nicodemus and Zohara's daughter
11. The Pharisee who wanted a private word with Jesus
12. The disciple who cut extra wood for the campsite
14. Who Jesus was helping prepare food in the kitchen

DOWN

2. The disciple who openly disagreed with Matthew joining the disciples
3. Who reported to Moses
4. Who apologized to Jesus for cutting his teaching short
6. Matthew's father
7. The Roman who visited Nicodemus and Zohara unannounced
10. The disciple who was very intelligent as a child
13. The disciple who went ahead of Jesus to prepare his secret meeting

Answer on page 158

Scrambled Message

Where Is Home?

When John asked Jesus if he wanted to roam about and not stay in one place he could call home, Jesus answered with this statement. Unscramble each word to see what he said.

T TWAN OT OD

EHT LIWL FO YM

ETFHRA . NDA I

WATN OT RPSEDA

HTE GAMESES FO

NVSLTOATA . OS

SEY 'I MA PYHAP

OT OTN TYAS NI

NEO LCEAP .

Answer on page 158

SECRET DECODER

Use the code below to unscramble what Jesus spoke to Nicodemus about.

✦	☸	❖	🕊	●	⚑	🐐	▢	✡	✝	⚷	✿	☾
A	B	C	D	E	F	G	H	I	J	K	L	M

◆	★	💰	◭	♪	☼	◗	❅	🗡	〜	✘	◎	※
N	O	P	Q	R	S	T	U	V	W	X	Y	Z

Answer on page 158

123

MAZE

SECRET MEETING

Help Jesus and
Nicodemus meet
on the rooftop.

Jesus

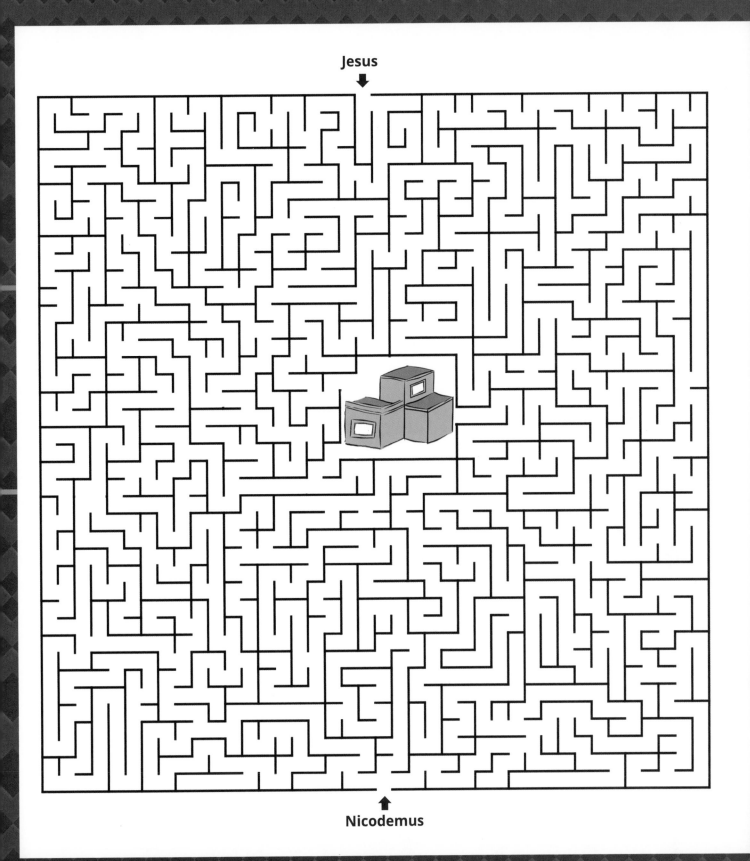

Nicodemus

When Jesus and Nicodemus were in their private meeting, Jesus spoke some very powerful words of hope and salvation. Find the words in the word search puzzle and then put them in order below to read what Jesus said.

_____

_____

_____

_____

BUT   IT   THROUGH
CONDEMN   IT   TO
DID   NOT   TO
GOD   SAVE   WORLD
HIM   SEND
HIS   SON
INTO   THE

```
        N   D   D   Q
    I   I   Q   O   O   L   O   I
    T   W   N   G   S   T   R   T
C   T   S   H   T   H   E   G   O   U
N   O   T   P   K   O   S   I   H   W
S   E   N   T   H   R   O   U   G   H
H   V   M   D   H   S   E   N   D   D
    A   T   P   E   I   P   Q   I
    S   E   U   O   M   M   D   W
        M   B   T   N
```

MIX AND MATCH

Match the definitions on the left with the words on the right.

What Jesus said he came to show people	Matthew
What Moses held up for the people to be healed	His parents
Why Zohara wanted to go back to Jerusalem	A dinner party
Who Quintus went to Nicodemus to talk about	His shop was robbed
Who Matthew went to visit	On a rooftop
Who did Jesus ask Thaddeus to cut extra wood for	The miracle worker
Why Nicodemus wanted to stay in Capernaum	The birth of a grandson
Where Jesus and Nicodemus met secretly	A weary traveler
What Jesus asked Mary to prepare	Unfinished work
Why Matthew's dad had to travel for work	A bronze serpent
The sick woman Simon tried to hide from Jesus	A kingdom
Who hosted the dinner party	A black cloak
What Jesus used as a disguise	Eden's mother

Answer on page 159

Jesus and Nicodemus recited a Scripture together at the end of thei
private meeting. Use the picture clues below to figure out what they said

 − DR + BL
add ED

 − H

_____   _____

− B

− S + W
remove E

_____   _____

− C + T

+ − J − D

_____   _____

− R + H

_____   _____

Answer on page 159

Alphabet practice!

Practice the next two letters of the Hebrew alphabet!

SHIN

This letter sounds like the **sh** in ship.

TAW

This letter sounds like the **t** in teach.

WORD CHANGE

S I C K

_ _ _ _ touch with tongue

_ _ _ _ hair bug

_ _ _ _ green citrus

_ _ _ _ ten-cent coin

_ _ _ _ circular structure

_ _ _ _ house

_ _ _ _ gap

_ _ _ _ grasp

_ _ _ _ shape into

_ _ _ _ gentle

_ _ _ _ grain building

_ _ _ _ going to

W E L L

Answer on page 159

SECRET DECODER

Use the code below to unscramble
what Shmuel told Nicodemus
about the Son of Man.

✦	☸	❖	🕊	●	⚑	🐕	□	✡	✝	🗝	✿	☽
A	B	C	D	E	F	G	H	I	J	K	L	M

◆	★	💰	▲	♫	☼	◉	✳	🗡	〰	✖	◎	※
N	O	P	Q	R	S	T	U	V	W	X	Y	Z

Answer on page 159

The notice posted by the Centurion was a warning for the Jewish people. What did it say?

Solve the equations and then use the numbers below to put the letters in place, so you can read the notice.

Posted Warning

A	B	C	D	E	F	G	H	I	J	K	L	M
1	2	3	4	5	6	7	8	9	10	11	12	13

N	O	P	Q	R	S	T	U	V	W	X	Y	Z
14	15	16	17	18	19	20	21	22	23	24	25	26

CODE

$\overline{6x3}$ $\overline{15\div3}$ $\overline{4x3}$ $\overline{3x3}$ $\overline{14\div2}$ $\overline{27\div3}$ $\overline{5x3}$ $\overline{7x3}$ $\overline{38\div2}$

$\overline{21\div3}$ $\overline{1x1}$ $\overline{10x2}$ $\overline{4x2}$ $\overline{20\div4}$ $\overline{9x2}$ $\overline{18\div2}$ $\overline{7x2}$ $\overline{28\div4}$ $\overline{19x1}$

$\overline{30\div2}$ $\overline{3x7}$ $\overline{5x4}$ $\overline{19\div1}$ $\overline{45\div5}$ $\overline{2x2}$ $\overline{25\div5}$ $\overline{5x4}$ $\overline{2x4}$ $\overline{10\div2}$

$\overline{1x19}$ $\overline{5x5}$ $\overline{28\div2}$ $\overline{1x1}$ $\overline{35\div5}$ $\overline{3x5}$ $\overline{63\div9}$ $\overline{7x3}$ $\overline{40\div8}$

$\overline{1\div1}$ $\overline{7x2}$ $\overline{16\div4}$ $\overline{64\div8}$ $\overline{30\div6}$ $\overline{14\div7}$ $\overline{3x6}$ $\overline{25\div5}$ $\overline{23x1}$

$\overline{1x19}$ $\overline{1x3}$ $\overline{2x4}$ $\overline{30\div2}$ $\overline{45\div3}$ $\overline{24\div2}$ $\overline{1x1}$ $\overline{3x6}$ $\overline{1x5}$

$\overline{1x19}$ $\overline{4x5}$ $\overline{6x3}$ $\overline{3x3}$ $\overline{1x3}$ $\overline{5x4}$ $\overline{4x3}$ $\overline{5x5}$

$\overline{4x4}$ $\overline{3x6}$ $\overline{3x5}$ $\overline{2x4}$ $\overline{45\div5}$ $\overline{1x2}$ $\overline{54\div6}$ $\overline{10x2}$ $\overline{20\div4}$ $\overline{16\div4}$

Answer on page 159

At the Well

Help Photina and Jesus meet at the well.

MIX AND MATCH

Match the definitions on the left with the words on the right.

The sign Nico's grandmother had over her door	Their nets
What Adonai El Roi means	To buy food
What Dasha asked if Jesus liked	To become a student
Why Matthew left tax collecting	Living water
Why Jesus visited Eden	The key to his house
Why Matthew left his dog	The God Who Sees Me
What Jesus said to Matthew	Adonai El Roi
What the disciples went into town for	Follow me
What Jesus said he had for Photina	To heal her mother
What Matthew left for his parents	Goat cheese
Where the marketplace Photina visited was	To protect his parents
What Simon and Andrew were going to sell	Sychar, Samaria

Answer on page 160

CROSSWORD FUN

Use the clues below to solve the crossword. Answers with more than one word are shown with brackets telling how many letters are in each word.

ACROSS

2. The disciple who said he wasn't a good runner
3. What was in the bundle left on the edge of the fountain
4. He wanted to accuse Jesus of false prophecy
5. The current husband of the woman at the well
6. He chose not to go with Jesus and the disciples
7. The name of the well where Jesus met the woman (6, 4)
11. Who Jesus met at the well
12. The first person to notice Simon's potential
13. The southernmost town in Galilee

DOWN

1. Who Jesus healed from a fever
2. The nationality of the woman at the well
3. He warned Matthew's parents about him being with Jesus
8. The fruit the woman at the well bought at the market
9. What Jesus asked the woman at the well for
10. The fruit the disciples were eating and passing along

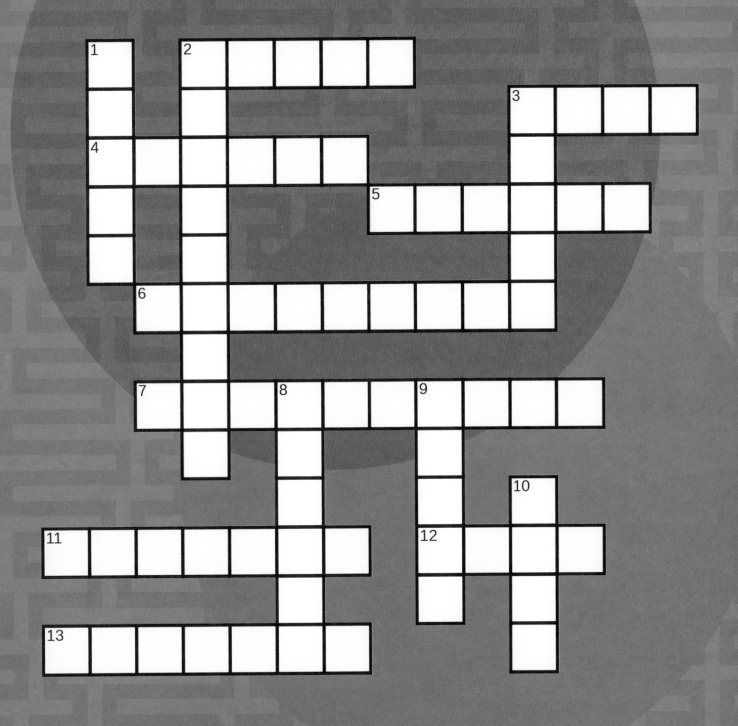

Answer on page 160

A Dinner Party

There were a lot of people and delicious food at the dinner party at Matthew's house! Find some of the guests, food, and decorations in the word search.

Andrew
Barnaby
Candles
Flatbread
Goat Cheese
Grapes
Jahaz
James
Jesus
John
Little James
Mary
Matthew
Nectarines

Oil Lamps
Olives
Pears
Pillows
Plates
Plums
Pomegranates
Rivka
Rom
Rugs
Rye Bread
Shula
Simon
Table

```
                              N H O J L P L X W I P N Q
                          V E G B M J Q G Y I Z R F
                        R W G K O Z S A L C E T D
                      R K E I X A T K A R I R T
                    P T R Z O T K A E M Y B L
                  F G D S I C M S B E O K E
                X Q N R L H B V R L M R J
              J A U L E F M B P E Z A
            R G P A E U N O M I S M Y
          G Y M S R A S P U Q E R
        S X P E W E M S L V S F F
        E S C H B U T H A C S P P
        M D A C L R J U T Y G C
        A Q A P W V E L E H R O
        J A K V I R B A S F A S
        Y X B E O F C P D L P W
        W D A I U Y Y O Q A E O
        O W R P Q E V M V T S L
        N K N P S U S E J B J L J
        M H A S I Z O G H R H I K
          H B W E M S R A E P P N
          X Y I E L Z A Z A A Z D R
            M O U H C N J D L C E B C
            G A F H T A N N S C O H J
              W S S S T E O E Z A H A J
                S G A E A N V M A I O L A
                  H U S S M I T E V I P X X J
                    R A E L S E N I R A T C E N
                      O J E M E D G C P I X N O
                        W B J S E L D N A C B Q M
```

Going in Circles

Write down each letter (in a clockwise spiral direction) to see what Jesus said about the water in the well. Cross out each letter after you pass through it. The arrows should help you get started.

E V E R

R W I L L Y

E R I N K S T O

T D W I L L G O H N

A R I E V E R T I F I E

W E T N A I N H V T R W

S V A L G ★ ★ I E H S H

I E H L A T S R H E T O

H O T I W M I W A D

T H R E T A G R

F W N I A I

O S K N

_ _ _ _ _ _ _ _ _ _ _ _ _ _

_ _ _ _ _ _ _ _ _ _ _ _

_ _ _ _ _ _ _ _ _.

_ _ _ _ _ _ _ _ _ _ _

_ _ _ _ _ _ _ _ _

_ _ _ _ _ _ _ _ _ _

_ _ _ _ _ _ _ _ _ _ _.

Answer on page 160

A SPECIAL PROMISE

Jesus shared a special promise with Photina. Use the pictures below to help you figure out his message.

 – M, O, R

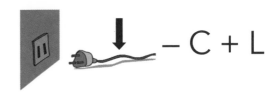 – C + L

_____

 + S

 – B + N

_____

2 – W

 – F, A, R

_____

 + ED

_____

BOUNTIFUL
HARVEST

USE THE LETTERS AND NUMBERS
TO SHOW WHERE EACH OF THESE
PIECES BELONG IN THE PUZZLE.
WE GOT YOU STARTED! ⟶ E8

_____

_____

_____

_____

_____

_____

_____

_____

Answer on page 160

Food for Thought

Jesus told the disciples what fed him more than real food. Figure out what his food was by following the paths from word to word to complete the sentence. Pass through each loaf of bread and don't travel on the same path more than once. Begin at the word "MY" and finish at the ★.

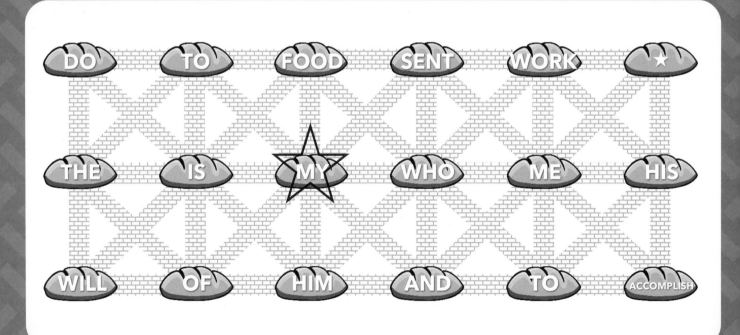

DO · TO · FOOD · SENT · WORK · ★

THE · IS · MY · WHO · ME · HIS

WILL · OF · HIM · AND · TO · ACCOMPLISH

Answer on page 160

ANSWER KEY

PAGE 4

E7	**A8**	**E4**
E5	**B7**	**F2**
C6	**D1**	**A4**

PAGE 7

Fear not, for I have redeemed you; I have called you by name, you are mine.

PAGE 9

Across – 3. Doll, 6. Tent, 8. Nicodemus, 9. Dove, 10. Key, 11. Fishing boat, 15. Caravan, 16. Zohara, 17. Isaiah, 18. Quintus

Down – 1. Lilith, 2. Eden, 4. Andrew, 5. Jehosaphat, 7. The Hammer, 12. Omar, 13. Papyrus, 14. Torah

PAGE 13

Booths in the market — Stalls
Wholesale traders — Merchants
Goods sold at the market — Wares
A round red fruit with edible seeds — Pomegranates
People buying goods at the market — Shoppers
Used to move and store market goods — Carts
They sit on the street asking for money — Beggars
Popular fruit smashed to make wine — Grapes
Another name for a market — Bazaar
Decorative floor coverings — Rugs
What Simon was trying to catch — Fish
Weaved containers — Baskets
Pear-shaped fruit often eaten dried — Figs
Typical warm climate footwear — Sandals
A woman's head covering — Scarf
A decorative accessory — Jewelry
Where liquids may be stored — Clay pots
A bag used to carry goods — Tote
Fruit used as a source of oil — Olives
Stall owner and seller of goods — Shopkeeper

PAGE 15

Crossword answers:

SHOPKEEPER, ZEALOT, SOLDIER, MAGISTRATE, PILATE, ROMAN, GREAT SANHEDRIN, TEACHER, CENTURION, PHARISEE

(Down words include: MERCHANT, FISHMONGER, STUDENT, JEW, JEWESS, PRIEST, SANDDUCEE, GUARD, VINEGROWER, TREASURER, SALO...)

PAGE 17

GARMENT
LECTERN
PARCHMENT
SCROLL
STALLS
WARES
TUNIC
BARRELS
HELMET
FRANKINCENSE
SANDALS
WAGON
TEFILLIN
LEDGER
LINEN
BUCKET
CARRIAGE

PAGE 19

Dove, Camel, Horse, Fish, Rats, Sardines, Pigs, Dog, Sheep, Rooster

PAGE 20

12 Bags

PAGE 23

Clue	Answer
the chief justice	Av Beit Din
commander of a Roman army	centurion
rules over a court	judge
grandmother	savta
Roman master	dominus
entertainer who keeps objects in the air	juggler
grandfather	saba
contracted tax collector	publicanus
a person who arranges or cuts hair	hairdresser
father	abba
a rabbi's wife	rabbanit
someone who can't see	blind person
like the Supreme Court of Jewish history	Sanhedrin
mother	eema

PAGE 24

E2   C3   E7

B8   C6   B4

E4   C1   A2

PAGE 27

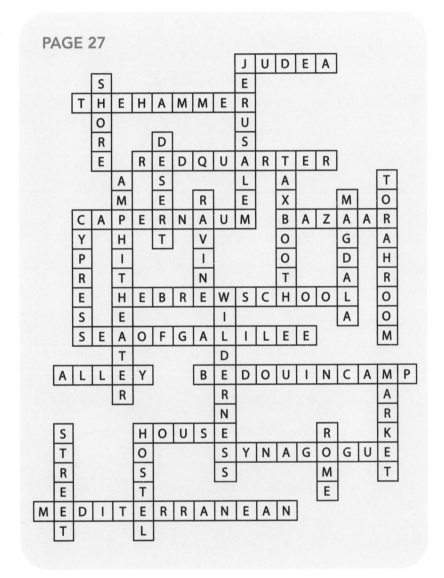

PAGE 29

Blessed are You, Lord our God, King of the universe, who created the fruit of the vine.

PAGE 31

1. Kiddush 2. Jasmine 3. Iris 4. Fruit 5. Candles 6. Shalom 7. Scarf 8. Dog 9. Students 10. Passover 11. Seder 12. First star 13. Weekly

PAGE 35

Across – 2. Joshua, 6. Lock & Key, 7. Decorations, 11. Sarah, 12. Chores, 15. Josiah

Down – 1. Bread, 3. Sleeping, 4. Dollhouse, 5. Peacemakers, 8. Abigail, 9. Father, 10. Pray, 13. Stream, 14. Toys

PAGE 36

Abigail, I know you can read. You are very special. This is for you. I did not come only for the wealthy.

PAGE 38

C1   F4   E2

C3   B5   E7

D6   A3   B7

Hear, Israel, the Lord is our God, the Lord is One. You shall love the Lord your God with all your heart, all your soul, and all your might. And it shall come to pass if you surely listen to the commandments that I command you today, that you may gather in your grain, your wine, and your oil, and you will eat and you will be satisfied. I am the Lord, your God, who led you from the land of Egypt to be a God to you. I am the Lord, your God. Amen.

CLAP, CLIP, CHIP, CHOP, COOP, COOL, FOOL, FOWL

God blessed the Seventh Day and made it holy, for on it He rested from all His work.

A person who builds with wood — C A R P E N T E R (7)

A person skilled in a craft — C R A F T S M A N (8)

A person with a lot of strength — S T R O N G M A N (4) (2)

A person who passes on knowledge — T E A C H E R (1)

A person who speaks for God — P R O P H E T (3)

A person who creates by joining items — B U I L D E R (5)

A person who kills someone — M U R D E R E R (6)

A person who breaks the law — C R I M I N A L

Who Abigail said Jesus was:

A G O O D M A N
1 2 3 4 5 6 7 8

N	I	W	Q	C	S	F	L	R	Y	A	X	O
1	2	3	4	5	6	7	8	9	10	11	12	13
J	E	U	D	V	K	B	T	G	Z	P	M	H
14	15	16	17	18	19	20	21	22	23	24	25	26

1. Show love to others.
2. Take God's Word and share it.
3. Honor your father and mother.
4. Love the Lord your God with all your heart.

CARP, CARE, FARE, FIRE, FORE, FORD, FOOD

ANDREW

```
T H E F R T S P I R I T X M O Y O F R L T
L M P T H E B U X N L O R D N L R I S P F
U P O N H R M E C B E C A U S E G R H E Q
W I H A S N X A N O I N T E D P L M E Q A
S T O L P R O C L A I M N R D L G O O D I
F H M N E W S R I Q N T O C G T H E P N R
P O O R L G H E C T H A S M R L S E N T P
S N T M E G R M S T T O B P R O C L A I M
T X L I B E R T Y I R L F T O B N T H E T
I C A P T I V E S R Y T E P D A N D F R L
P H R M O L R E C O V E R I N G T S O F R
S I G H T E Q P R L T O L M T H E T C L P
R C H B L I N D N H T P T O Q R S S E T P
U A T V H L I B E R T Y W A B T H O S E B
W H O Q R T H S A R E L N P R N Q T H L S
C T X O P P R E S S E D T B L T O S F R Q
A B D M C P R T F A P R O C L A I M T P O
G T H E Q N G Y E A R L T F I O F H R L M
T H E B T L O R D S C H R F A V O R T X F
```

PAGE 58

C4   E7   B6

D2   D6   A3

F5   B1   E4

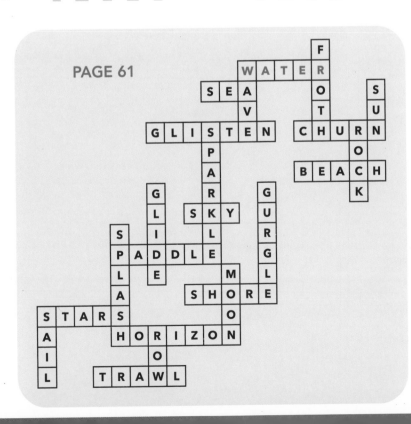

PAGE 61

PAGE 63

WISH, WASH,
MASH, MAST,
MOST, MOAT,
MEAT, MEAL

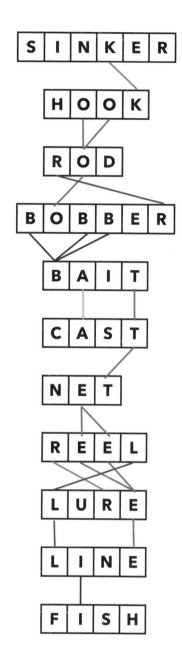

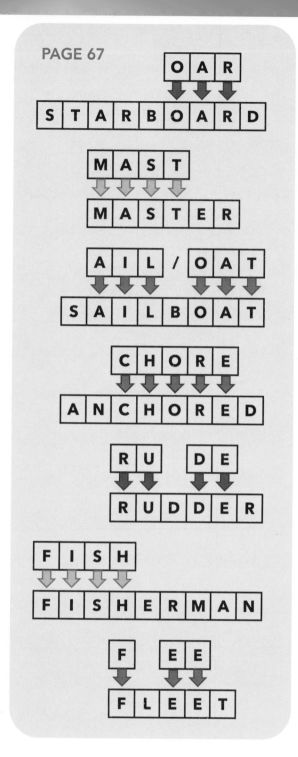

PAGE 69

Across – 2. Forty, 3. Lure, 5. Messiah, 8. Follow me, 9. Ear, 12. John the Baptist, 13. Zebedee

Down – 1. Bobber, 3. Lamb of God, 4. Wheel, 6. Quintus, 7. Traitor, 10. Zero, 11. Matthew 14. Dog

PAGE 71

WAGER, WAGE, WADE, WIDE

PAGE 72

Wilderness

Simon—CUCUMBER,
Andrew—LENTILS,
Thaddeus—PITA,
Mary—OLIVES,
James—FISH,
John—GRAPES,
Big James—SALAD,
Jesus—LAMB

C6	E7	B8
E5	C4	A2
D3	F4	B5

Across – 3. Abijah, 6. Scholars,
8. Joseph, 9. Jerusalem
12. Rabbi, 13. Temple, 14. Feast

Down – 1. Caravan, 2. Father,
4. Teaching, 5. Passover,
7. Three, 10. Scribe, 11. Mary
14. Twelve

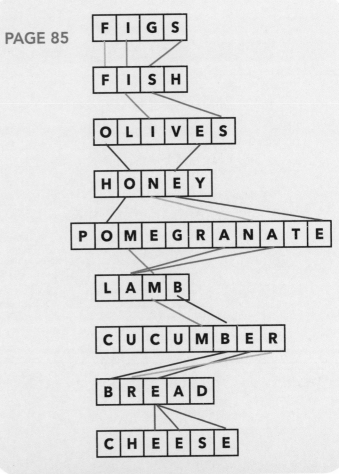

PAGE 91

Who has ascended into heaven and come down?
Who has gathered the wind in his fists?
Who has wrapped up the waters in a garment?
Who has established all the ends of the earth?

PAGE 93

LAKE, MAKE, MALE, MALL, WALL

PAGE 94

F6	E7	E1
D8	B7	B2
D3	A5	C5

PAGE 97

Across – 3. Simon, 4. Joshua,
7. Dasha, 9. Thaddeus,
11. Carpenter, 14. Matthew,
15. Roof

Down – 1. Mason, 2. James,
5. Abigail, 6. Paralytic,
8. Andrew, 10. Salome,
12. Tamar, 13. Leper

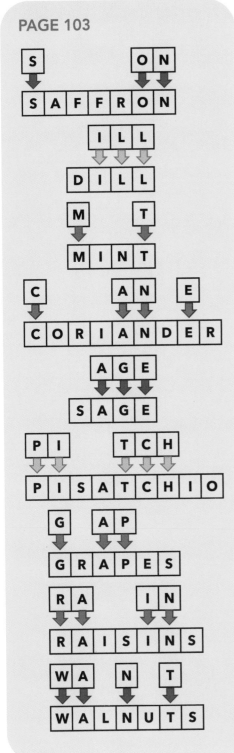

A	B	C	D	E	F	G	H	I	J	K	L	M
5	14	10	18	2	25	19	11	3	21	16	23	24

N	O	P	Q	R	S	T	U	V	W	X	Y	Z
8	20	6	17	1	12	7	22	13	9	26	15	24

Neither the angels in heaven nor the Son of Man know the day or the hour, but only the Father. So you must always be ready.

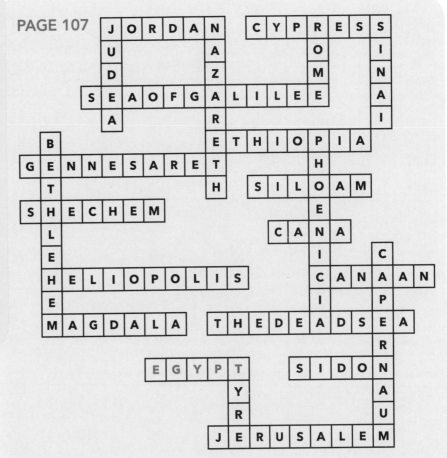

PAGE 109

Big words don't matter to God. It's better to go into your room and shut the door and pray to your Father who sees in secret.

PAGE 110

Consider how the wild flowers grow. They do not labor or spin. Yet I tell you, not even King Solomon dressed as beautifully. If that is how God clothes the grass of the field, which is here today, and tomorrow is thrown into the fire, how much more will he clothe you?

HIDDEN MESSAGE:
God loves you more than you can imagine. He will take good care of you.

PAGE 112

Our faith isn't something that we hide and keep to ourselves.
You are the light of the world.
A city on a hill cannot be hidden.

PAGE 115

BEAD, BEND, BAND, BALD, BALL, WALL, WALE, WILE, WIFE

PAGE 116

B3   E5   D4

D6   F3   A5

B7   B1   D2

PAGE 119

Across – 1. Moses, 3. John, 5. Gaius, 8. Isabel, 9. Havilah, 11. Nicodemus, 12. Thaddeus, 14. Eden

Down – 2. Simon, 3. Joshua, 4. Mary, 6. Alphaeus, 7. Quintus, 10. Matthew, 13. Andrew

PAGE 121

I want to do the will of my Father. And I want to spread the message of salvation. So yes, I am happy to not stay in one place.

PAGE 123

God loves the world in this way… that he gave his only Son, that whoever believes in him should not perish but have eternal life.

PAGE 126

God did not send his Son into the world to condemn it, but to save it through him.

What Jesus said he came to show people — Matthew

What Moses held up for the people to be healed — His parents

Why Zohara wanted to go back to Jerusalem — A dinner party

Who Quintus went to Nicodemus to talk about — His shop was robbed

Who Matthew went to visit — On a rooftop

Who did Jesus ask Thaddeus to cut extra wood for — The miracle worker

Why Nicodemus wanted to stay in Capernaum — The birth of a grandson

Where Jesus and Nicodemus met secretly — A weary traveler

What Jesus asked Mary to prepare — Unfinished work

Why Matthew's dad had to travel for work — A bronze serpent

The sick woman Simon tried to hide from Jesus — A kingdom

Who hosted the dinner party — A black cloak

What Jesus used as a disguise — Eden's mother

PAGE 129

Blessed are all who take refuge in him.

PAGE 131

LICK, LICE, LIME, DIME, DOME, HOME, HOLE, HOLD, MOLD, MILL, WILL

PAGE 133

His dominion is an everlasting dominion, which shall not pass away, and his kingdom one that shall not be destroyed.

PAGE 135

Religious gatherings outside the synagogue and Hebrew school are strictly prohibited.

PAGE 139

Across – 2. Simon, 3. Gold, 4. Shmuel, 5. Neriah, 6. Nicodemus, 7. Jacob's Well, 12. Eden, 13. Jezreel

Down – 1. Dasha, 2. Samaritan, 3. Gaius, 8. Orange, 9. Water, 10. Pear

PAGE 143

Everyone who drinks of this water will thirst again. Whoever drinks of the water that I will give him will never thirst again.

PAGE 145

The Lord is near to the brokenhearted.

PAGE 146

E6	D4	C5
E3	C7	A5
B3	B1	C2

PAGE 148

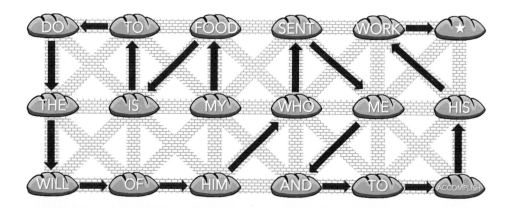